the best of
Barenaked Ladies

Be My Yoko Ono

Words and Music by
STEVEN PAGE and ED ROBERTSON

2

8

Box Set

Words and Music by
STEVEN PAGE

Bossa nova ♩ = 90

Intro:

20

CCC128

Brian Wilson

Words and Music by
STEVEN PAGE

28

I'm ly-ing in bed ___ just like Bri-an Wil-son did, ___

2nd time to Coda ⊕

whoah. ___

Bridge:

And if you want to find me I'll be

34

CCC128

Enid

Words and Music by
STEVEN PAGE and ED ROBERTSON

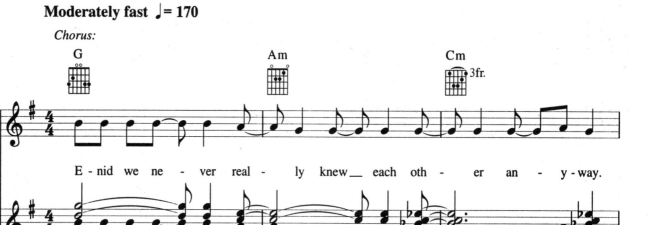

Verse 1:

42

I took a beat - ing when you wrote me those let - ters,

And ev - 'ry time___ I re - mem-bered the

taste of___ your lip___ gloss.

Chorus:

E - nid we ne - ver real -

CCC128

If I Had $1,000,000

Words and Music by
STEVEN PAGE and ED ROBERTSON

54

CCC128

58

What A Good Boy

Words by
STEVEN PAGE

Music by
STEVEN PAGE and ED ROBERTSON

64

CCC128

66

68

70

Alternative Girlfriend

Words and Music by
STEPHEN DUFFY and STEVEN PAGE

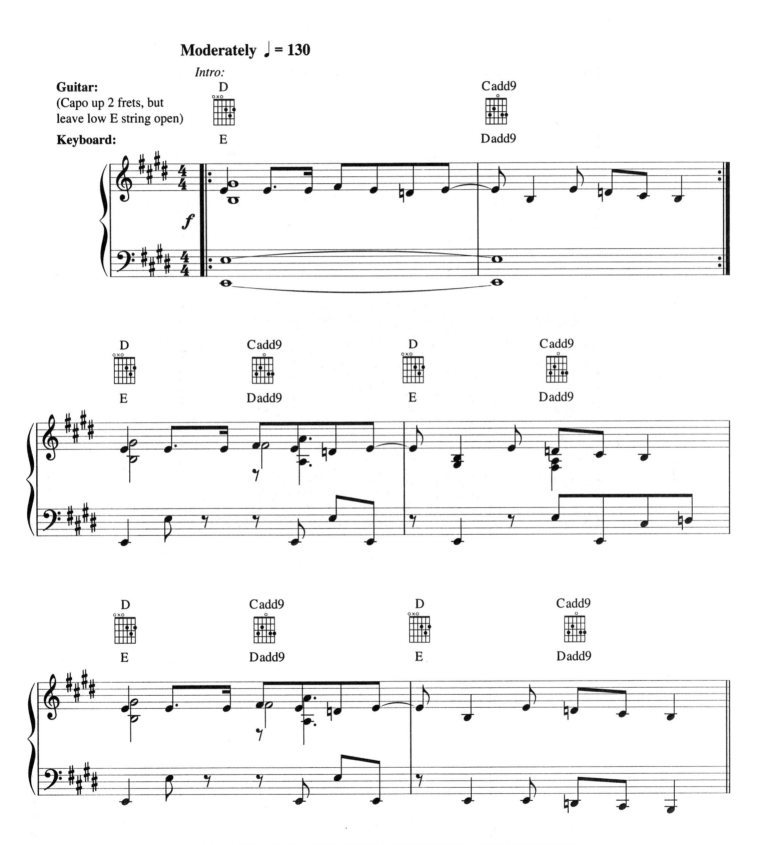

78

CCC128

86

Jane

Words and Music by
STEPHEN DUFFY and STEVEN PAGE

92

CCC128

geth - er, is what I can not ex - plain to _____ Jane.

D.S. al Coda

Tag:

⊕ *Coda*

Jane, _____ come on. _____

CCC128

94

Life, In A Nutshell

Words and Music by
STEVEN PAGE and ED ROBERTSON

CCC128

102

CCC128

mat - ters to me____ is she.____

The Old Apartment

Words and Music by
STEVEN PAGE & ED ROBERTSON

CCC128

108

CCC128

Shoe Box

Words by
STEVEN PAGE & ED ROBERTSON

Music by
STEVEN PAGE

Rock ♩ = 152

Verse 1:

1. A key in the door,____ a step on the floor,____ A note on the ta-

-ble and a meal in the mi - cro. Note says, "I'm in bed,____ please make sure that you're fed. __

112

CCC128

114

Straw Hat And Old Dirty Hank

Words and Music by
STEVEN PAGE & ED ROBERTSON

126

CCC128

know it was meant to be this way, I know it was meant to be this

way.

This Is Where It Ends

Words and Music by
STEVEN PAGE & ED ROBERTSON

132

don't _ want the re - spon-si - bil -i - ty of prov- ing its im - por - tance.

Coda

This is where it ends.

CCC128

Discography

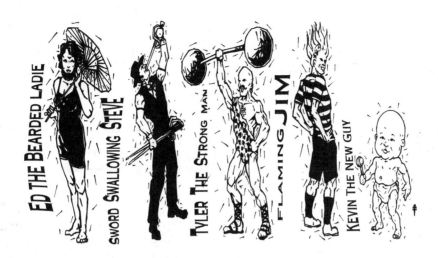

ALBUMS

BUCK NAKED (1989) – Cassette (Canada) Independent Release

BARENAKED LUNCH (1990) – Cassette (Canada) Page Publications

BARENAKED LADIES (1991) – Cassette (Canada) Page Publications

VARIETY RECORDINGS: BARENAKED LADIES (1991) – CD (Canada)
Canadian Broadcasting Corporation

GORDON (1992) – CD and Cassette (North America) Sire/Reprise

MAYBE YOU SHOULD DRIVE (1994) – CD and Cassette (North America) Sire/Reprise

BORN ON A PIRATE SHIP (1995) – Enhanced CD and Cassette (North America)
Sire/Reprise

ROCK SPECTACLE (1996) – Enhanced CD and Cassette (North America) Sire/Reprise

SINGLES

Enid (1992) – CD (England) Sire/Reprise
Enid (1992) – Cassette (US) Sire/Reprise

Brian Wilson (1993) – CD (England) Sire/Reprise
Brian Wilson (1993) – Cassette (US) Sire/Reprise

If I Had $1,000,000 (1993) – CD (England) Sire/Reprise

Be My Yoko Ono (1993) – Cassette (US) Sire/Reprise

Jane (1994) – CD (England) Sire/Reprise
Jane (1994) – Cassette (US) Sire/Reprise

Alternative Girlfriend (1995) – CD (US) Sire/Reprise

Shoe Box (1996) – Enhanced CD (North America) Sire/Reprise

If I Had $1,000,000 (1996) – CD (England) Sire/Reprise

The Old Apartment (1997) – CD and Cassette (North America) Sire/Reprise

Credits

Barenaked Ladies are

Jim Creeggan
Kevin Hearn
Steven Page
Ed Robertson
Tyler Stewart

Contact Address
Management; Nettwerk Productions,
Box 330-1755 Robson St.,
Vancouver, B.C., Canada V6G 3B7
Tel (604) 654-2929 **Fax** (604) 654-1993
E-Mail info@nettmanagement.com
Compuserve 74777,547
Nett Webb URL http://www.nettwerk.com/

For the Official Barenaked Ladies World Wide Web Site, check out
http://www.RepriseRec.com/BarenakedLadies
and for the Unofficial (but very cool) Fan Site, check out
http://www.FisherTowne.com/Barenaked/

Music Arranged by Dan Parr;
with the assistance of Jim Creeggan and Ed Robertson

Book Design and Layout by Isabel Preto, Crystal Heald, and Alexandria Stuart

Contents Imagery Key
* Photos courtesy Jay Blakesburg
† Photos courtesy Andrew MacNaughtan
‡ Photos/Images courtesy Neil Prime-Coote — Atire

Cover Imagery

Front: † high contrast band photo
‡ band with sandwich photo; treasure map illustration
* fuchsia background photo; white background photo

Spine: † pictures of individual band members taken from group photo

Back: ‡ astronaut band photo
* smiling band photo